700
RUB

Rubin, Susan
Goldman.

Art against the
odds.

$21.99

000044011
09/09/2004

DATE			

against.

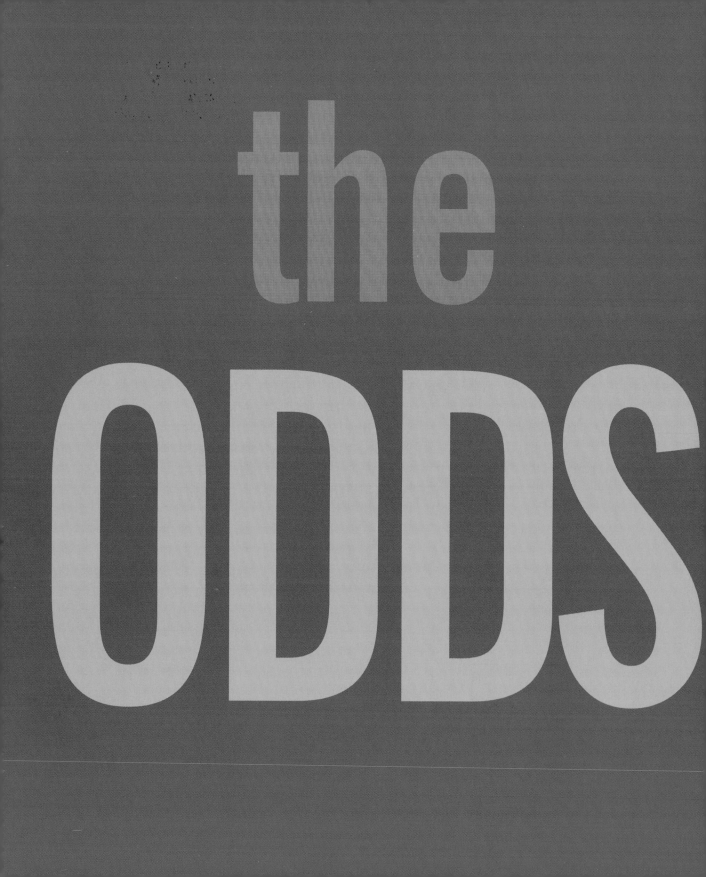

From SLAVE QUILTS to PRISON PAINTINGS

By Susan Goldman Rubin

CROWN PUBLISHERS ♛ NEW YORK

To my sons John and Peter, with love

Library of Congress Cataloging-in-Publication Data
Rubin, Susan Goldman.
Art against the odds : from slave quilts to prison paintings / Susan Goldman Rubin. — 1st ed.
p. cm.
Includes bibliographical references and index.
ISBN 0-375-82406-5 (trade) — ISBN 0-375-92406-X (lib. bdg.)
1. Outsider art — United States — Juvenile literature. I. Title.
N6505.5.O87 R83 2004
700'.9'045—dc21
2003012139

Printed in the United States of America
March 2004
10 9 8 7 6 5 4 3 2 1
First Edition

"**Just look at your artwork. . . . Only someone with a strong life force could possibly have created that.**"

—from *Whirligig* by Paul Fleischman

acknowledgments

For me this book began with my friend and fellow author Kathleen Krull and a chance meeting at a California Reading Association conference. I thank Kathy for putting me in touch with my wonderful editor, Nancy Hinkel. It has been a joy to work with Nancy and her assistant editor Jamie Weiss, designer Kate Gartner and art director Isabel Warren-Lynch, and the rest of the staff at Random House Children's Books. It was Kate who read the obituary of Miné Okubo in the first place and had the idea of doing a book on this theme.

In the course of research, many people helped me. I especially want to thank Dr. John Schultz, Nancy Fast, Toni Radler, and Sharon Carter at the Christian Children's Fund; Tim Rollins; my friend Helga Weissová; my dear friend Fama Mor, the former archivist at the Simon Wiesenthal Center—Museum of Tolerance; and my brother and sister-in-law, Ed and Patti Moldof, who took me to an exhibit at the Virginia Historical Society, where I first saw the drawings of Private Robert K. Sneden.

As always, I am indebted to my circle of writing friends, who gave advice and cheered me on. I thank my husband, Michael, for his loving support, and my son Andy and my grandson Marty for their superb technical assistance. But I am most grateful to George Nicholson for his guidance, enthusiasm, and steadfast belief in the importance of art books for young readers.

contents

foreword

by Helga Weissová, as told to the author on May 6, 2003

Art was very important to me when I was at Terezin because when [I was] drawing, it was my own world. Nobody could interrupt it or step inside. It was my privacy. There was no privacy for anybody at Terezin. We were pressed together. It helped me to fly over the terrible reality into another world. I drew my dreams, my hopes, and my wishes. I imagined my future. We [my friend Franzi and I] spoke about the future at night. We shall be mothers. We shall have children. We even had names for our children and the clothes they would wear. It was a kind of play. It helped me to run away and escape from a terrible reality into my own private world. I could do what I wanted in drawing. We were not free. Orders. Orders. At the time I was drawing, I forgot what was happening. I felt free.

introduction

introduction

In life people take risks and strive to accomplish goals even
though the chances, or odds, of success are slight. This book looks at
children and adults who felt compelled to make different kinds of art
despite living under the most awful conditions—imprisonment, war,
poverty, racism, and illness. In other words, they created art "against the
odds." They felt an inner urge to express themselves, not always thinking of their work as art. Yet others perceived it as such. These artists
escaped into their art as they created and, in the process, found relief
and pleasure.

Many of them had little or no training. Or encouragement. They
had to scrounge for materials. Even though they were locked out of
the mainstream, they produced works of art that convey powerful
emotions of joy and anger, and even reflect a sense of humor. Many of
these artworks have historical significance as well. The artists may be
unknown or forgotten, but their works live on.

chapter 1
Outsider Art

In 1972, a British art historian, Roger Cardinal, coined the term "outsider art." By this he meant artwork created by "outsiders"—criminals, spiritualists (who believed they communicated with the dead), psychiatric patients, and even contemporary folk artists. All of these people shared certain traits: they were self-taught, were isolated from the rest of the world, and cared nothing about showing their work publicly. Yet their creations displayed such originality, power, and beauty that they inspired professional artists. Scholars and critics became particularly fascinated with "insane art," produced by people struggling with mental illness.

HENRY DARGER

Henry Darger, a janitor and dishwasher from Chicago, never had art lessons. No one taught him how to draw or paint. But Darger needed to make pictures and write long stories in order to live in his private world. So he invented his own methods and kept his work a secret, never showing it to anyone. Darger is regarded as the most important self-taught American artist of the twentieth century. Many critics consider him a genius for his marvelous use of color and the immensity of his output.

Yet because of his appearance and behavior, some people thought

he was crazy or even mentally retarded. Darger suffered from a mental illness called schizophrenia. He saw things that weren't really there and heard imaginary voices. "My neighbors were quite upset when they realized that Henry was going to stay," recalled his neighbor and landlord, photographer Nathan Lerner. Darger was short, only five feet one inch tall, and bald, and he had a bushy mustache. He wore shabby clothes that were too big for him. He didn't like to take baths and smelled bad. In winter he went around wearing a long, dirty, greasy coat.

"People told me of seeing Henry on the street talking to himself," recalled Lerner. "I never saw him talking to himself, but I heard him in the hallway all the time. He'd be either singing or talking to somebody."

Darger had no friends or family. No one came to visit him. "While he seemed a lonely man without friends during the day," remembered Lerner, "at night when he entered his room, his loneliness must have vanished. He was in his own world of imagination, surrounded by all of his creations."

Biographers believe Darger's art

stemmed from his troubled childhood. "I don't know of anyone who has overcome so many difficulties and problems," said Lerner.

Darger was born on April 12, 1892, in Chicago, although he later claimed to have come from Germany, his father's birthplace, or even Brazil. His mother died giving birth to a baby girl just days before Darger turned four, and the baby was immediately put up for adoption. Darger never recovered from his grief. "I lost my sister by adoption," he wrote. "I never knew or seen her, or knew her name." From that

*Henry Darger, **Untitled** (idyllic landscape with children). Darger based this unusual painting on figures he copied from coloring books.* [Collection American Folk Art Museum, New York]

moment on, Darger tried to replace his sister by creating imaginary little girls, and he remained a child himself. "I hated to see the day come when I will be grown up," he wrote in his old age. "I wished to be young always."

After his mother's death, Darger lived in Chicago with his father, whom he described as "a tailor and a kind and easygoing man." His father brought home newspapers that they enjoyed together, and Darger learned how to read. However, in 1900,

Darger's father became too ill to take care of him and sent him to a Catholic boys' home. The other kids gave him the nickname Crazy because he made funny noises in his throat and moved his hands in strange gestures. Darger kept hoping his father would come and get him, but when his father died in 1905, the boy was placed in the Illinois Asylum for Feeble-Minded Children. A doctor had completely misdiagnosed him, saying, "Little Henry's heart is not in the right place."

After a while Darger grew

accustomed to the routine of the asylum and felt comfortable there. "Finally I got to like the place," he wrote, "and the meals were good and plenty." By the time he became a teenager, though, he wanted to get out. Darger tried to escape a few times, only to return to the familiarity of the asylum. But when he was sixteen, he ran away and never went back.

Darger supported himself by working in a series of Catholic hospitals, scrubbing floors on his hands and knees. He lived alone

Henry Darger, study of girl and "Blengin." Darger repeated this little girl in a polka-dot dress five times in the idyllic landscape with children shown on pages 2 and 3, and when he added curved horns to her head, she became a creature he called a Blengin.
[Collection American Folk Art Museum, New York]

in a large rented room on the second floor of an apartment house in downtown Chicago and stayed there for forty years.

"His room was filled from floor to ceiling with the debris of his scavenging," recalled Lerner. "He would take long walks in order to gather his amazing collections, and at great distances from home he could be seen poking through garbage with his cane, looking for his treasures. Crucifixes, broken toys, old magazines, scores of used eyeglasses repaired with tape, hundreds of balls of twine that he made by tying small pieces together . . . the list was endless." Sometimes Lerner heard Darger carrying on conversations all by himself, making up the different voices. "At other times he would sing strange songs, perhaps in Portuguese, inasmuch as he claimed to be Brazilian."

Lerner didn't know that Darger was creating an enormous body of work. He not only kept diaries and a six-volume weather journal comparing the weather with official forecasts each day for eleven years, but he wrote an autobiography and his own myth: *The Story of the Vivian Girls, in What Is Known as the Realms of the Unreal.* The epic saga told of the adventures of seven little sisters who heroically fought against adult "Glandelinians" to free enslaved children. Darger thought of himself as a guardian and protector of children. He began the fantasy when he was nineteen years old and wrote it in longhand, then typed it, and illustrated it with hundreds of colorful scroll-like paintings. Many scrolls depict violent battles. Others reflect quiet moments, with the little girls lined up in a bizarre landscape.

Darger taught himself how to draw and paint by studying comic books, magazines, and children's coloring books that he bought at the corner drugstore. Usually he traced the figures he needed for his composition. If the figures were not the right size, he reduced or enlarged them at the drugstore's photography counter. Often he simply cut out pictures and pasted them onto his watercolor paintings, making a collage.

Much of Darger's art contains questionable content—nude figures that shock and disturb some viewers. But he created these images to portray his private fantasy world, never intending to exhibit them. Just before Darger died on April 13, 1973, one day after his eighty-first birthday, Lerner discovered his work. Lerner was astonished! As a photographer and artist himself, he recognized Darger's work as art. "It is a humbling experience now to have to admit that not until I looked under all the debris in his room did I become aware of the incredible world that Henry had created from within himself," Lerner said. He established a study center to make Darger's writings, drawings, and paintings available to the public. The pictures have been shown in museums worldwide as a prime example of American outsider art. Today Darger's work is preserved and displayed in the American Folk Art Museum in New York City.

ADOLF WÖLFLI

One of the first people to be recognized as an outsider artist was Adolf Wölfli. A barrel-chested man with muscular arms, Wölfli spent most of his life at Waldau Mental Asylum near Bern, Switzerland. There he created an astounding body of artwork, poetry, and musical compositions. Like Darger, Wölfli suffered from schizophrenia, seeing visions of another world and hearing voices that didn't really exist. And like Darger, he had experienced a miserable childhood.

He was born in Bowil, Canton Bern, Switzerland, on March 1, 1864, the youngest of seven children. Two of his brothers, also named Adolf, died in infancy. His father, a stonecutter and alcoholic, deserted the family when Wölfli was about five years old. His mother tried to support them by raising vegetables and flowers and working in a laundry. "For a long time we had scarcely anything to eat," wrote Wölfli. When she could no longer take care of them, the family split up and Wölfli went to live with foster parents on a farm. "No one

Adolf Wölfli in his cell at Waldau Mental Asylum, 1921. Wölfli points to one of his compositions.

can imagine the trouble and hardship I had to struggle against as a farmer's apprentice," Wölfli wrote. "I had to guard 28 to 30 goats for my foster parents and those I chased every morning." But he enjoyed the countryside. "I saw alpine roses and buttercups daily," he wrote, "and the views into the distance were absolutely enchanting." In 1873, when he was eight years old, Wölfli's mother died. For the next few years he lived with different families as a farmhand and was treated badly.

Adolf Wölfli, **Holy St. Adolf Tower,** 1919. Wölfli repeated rows of weird masked faces peering at the viewer. He drew this picture with graphite and colored pencil. [Collection American Folk Art Museum, New York]

the romance. Wölfli was crushed. "That same evening, burning with grief over my lost love," he wrote, "I rolled in the snow and wept bitterly over being so cruelly deprived of my happiness."

Wölfli moved to the city of Bern and worked as a handyman and grave digger. Following some unhappy romances, he was found guilty of a crime and was sent to prison. After his release, his behavior grew stranger. In 1895, he attempted another crime and was caught and sent to Waldau Mental Asylum. Doctors examined him and declared him a danger to society. So at age thirty-one, Wölfli was locked up for good.

At first he had violent outbursts and spent most of his time in solitary confinement. But in 1899, Wölfli began drawing pictures and seemed to calm down. "He is allowed to draw," wrote the doctors, "and gets every week a new pencil." Soon they wrote, "He uses up a pencil every 2 to 3 days. . . . His drawings are always the same fantastic jumble, yet his skill in drawing straight lines or simple curves without drawing

Then, at age sixteen, he fell in love with a rich farmer's daughter and wanted to marry her. But her parents found out and broke up

equipment is admirable." Wölfli filled sheets of paper with elaborate designs of swirling ovals, rings, and bands that often enclosed numbers and letters, such as his own initials, A and W.

In 1907, Dr. Walter Morgenthaler, a psychiatrist, met Wölfli and became deeply interested in his life and artwork. Wölfli told Morgenthaler about his early years and said that the thousands of pictures he drew showed imaginary adventures that had taken place before his mother's death. These were "lost memories," Wölfli explained. In his art Wölfli stepped into another world that existed only for him. And in this fantasy place he saw himself transformed as St. Adolf.

Morgenthaler gave Wölfli colored pencils, with which he produced a landscape from memory, *Felsenau, Bern, 1907.* The picture—showing houses, a cotton mill, and a stream bordered by a fence—glows with shades of orange, yellow, deep green, and blue, combined with black and gray pencil.

Morgenthaler observed Wölfli at work and described his tech-

Adolf Wölfli, **The Kander Valley in the Bernese Oberland,** *1926. Wölfli drew this picture with graphite and colored pencil on paper.* [Collection American Folk Art Museum, New York]

nique. Using big sheets of paper, he started drawing at the edges to complete a border, then moved inward toward the center until the entire sheet was filled. In many drawings Wölfli repeated an odd masked face that represented himself as a prisoner. His complex designs included grotesque figures, women's shoes, birds, plants, snails, animals, and even musical notes. He also composed sixteen books of music and performed his own compositions on a horn made of rolled-up paper.

In 1921, Morgenthaler published a study called *Madness and Art: The Life and Works of Adolf Wölfli.* It was the first time a patient was considered an artist rather than just someone mentally ill. Morgenthaler appreciated the high quality of Wölfli's draftsmanship and his unique vision. These were not just crazy drawings but a sequence of shapes and patterns developed from one picture to the next.

*Adolf Wölfli, **Campbell's Tomato Soup**, 1929. In this collage Wölfli combined pictures cut from magazines with his own writings.*

Morgenthaler wrote about Wölfli's daily routine. "He gets up at six o'clock with the other patients, gets dressed extremely slowly.... He makes his own bed and sometimes waxes the floor of his cell. He does not care much for grooming himself.... After he gets dressed, he waits for his breakfast, and chatting animat-edly with his voices, he paces up and down the hall." After eating breakfast, Wölfli returned to his cell and drew for the whole day until it got dark, stopping briefly just to eat meals.

Like Henry Darger, Wölfli often cut pictures and advertise-ments out of magazines and pasted them onto his paper for a collage. For example, *Chocolat Suchard,* 1918, from *Book with Songs and Dances,* includes an ad for chocolate as well as one for watches. These fit together like puzzle pieces alongside a boot. And within the boot there are stylized birds and more musical notes, part of one of Wölfli's own scores. Two other composi-tions, *Delicious Tomato Soup* and *Campbell's Tomato Soup,* 1929, fea-ture bowls of steaming red soup taken from English-language mag-azines and attached alongside Wölfli's handwritten jottings.

Over the course of thirty-five years in the asylum, Wölfli con-tinued working on his immense autobiographical projects. At the time of his death in 1930, he was not finished. However, the col-lection of work he left behind is regarded as a masterpiece and belongs to the Museum of Fine Arts in Bern.

Wölfli and Darger were both schizophrenics. But many out-sider artists suffer from other mental disorders, such as autism and depression. Idiot savants, for example, possess exceptional tal-ent in the fields of art, music, and mathematics.

In recent years outsider art has become increasingly popular with collectors. Works originally meant to remain secret are sold at prestigious auction houses. And since 1982, an annual Outsider Art Fair has been held in the Puck Building in New York City.

chapter 2
Captured

Most people go to jail because they have committed crimes.
Others may be caught by an enemy during a war. And there are those
who are held captive simply as a result of circumstances beyond their
control. Through the years, prisoners have coped with their ordeals
and sustained hope by creating art.

BEHIND BARS: PRISON ART

Jailed criminals live in ugly surroundings. Bars, chains, and wire fences
enclose them. Cement walls and ceilings have no color. Toilets and
sinks are steel gray. Occasionally a prisoner spots a bit of color and is
thrilled.

"I was walking the yard, admiring the beautiful colors of the dis-
tant foliage," remembered convict Ronnie White. "They were really
brilliant and freed my mind for a spell. I looked down and found this
leaf and looked at it in awe. . . . I stuck it in my sock and brought it
back to my cell feeling like I had something special. It was the only
leaf I could find in the whole yard."

White had been in and out of jails since he was a teenager. At age
fifteen he dropped out of school in Fall River, Massachusetts, because
he had been held back in sixth grade while all his friends went on
to junior high. From then on he spent his time hanging out at a pool

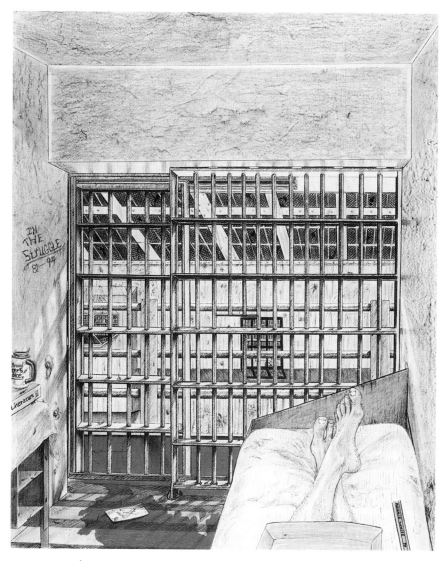

Ronnie White, **Essex III #39 Walpole.** *White shows the view from his bunk—bars beyond lock him in. He is still serving time in prison.*

from the monotonous, often frightening life. Through his art he felt more human. White's drawing titled *Essex III #39 Walpole* is a depiction of his small cell in maximum security.

Some prisoners reveal their struggle between good and evil impulses in their art. "Painting kept me from hurting a whole bunch of people," said Steven Ainsworth, a prisoner on death row. Ainsworth lived in isolation, unable to see other prisoners or talk to them. He could only leave his cell in handcuffs a few times a week to exercise. His drawing *What's Going On Out There?* illustrates how he coped. The realistic picture, composed of delicate black dots, shows his hand extended through the bars of his cell. He holds a rectangular piece of metal that reflects the eye and nose of the prisoner in the next cell.

Art served as a kind of therapy for Charles Mosby. "There's times I'm under a lot of aggravation and I feel like, you know, hitting somebody," he said. "But instead I can sit there and draw something, and while I'm drawing I can let my mind flow." An

hall. By the time he was seventeen he was imprisoned on charges of burglary, car theft, and shoplifting.

Like many prisoners, White began drawing and painting while in jail and discovered his talent only *after* he had committed crimes. He bought art supplies— paper, pencils, ballpoint pens, and crayons—in the canteen. Art helped White escape mentally

alcoholic at age twelve, Mosby was imprisoned by the time he was thirteen. He wanted to hurt other people. "I'm locked up because of my stupidity, self-hatred, and alcoholism," he admitted. But art helped him to survive and change. "I turned to drawing because life here is very

Arthur Keigney, **Walpole, 1972.** *Keigney depicted life behind bars during a brief incarceration at the Massachusetts state prison at Walpole, showing prisoners doing everything from injecting drugs to reading books.*

Crystal Stimpson, **My World.** *Stimpson's face is cut from a photograph and pasted onto the acrylic painting.*

boring and depressing," he said, "and also a serious threat to my sanity. I had to find something to ease my mind."

Mosby painted vividly colored pictures of life on the outside from his imagination. While doing routine prison jobs, he kept thinking about painting. "All I have to do is look inside my mind and be creative," he said. "I can open my eyes and see beauty and colors, like I always used to think my skin was just dark brown but I can see now I am a variety of color." Some of

his pictures, such as *It's Spring,* convey a cheerful mood. Others make a sad statement. In *Where Have All the Boys Gone?* the heads of two tearful women float above a graveyard filled with tombstones of men and boys, ages twelve to twenty-one, who have been killed by drugs and guns.

Prisoners often portray scenes of their everyday life behind bars. Arthur Keigney started carrying a gun and holding up banks when he was just a teenager. "I have been incarcerated since 1971 for masked armed bank

robbery and possession of a machine gun," he said in 1990. In prison Keigney became interested in art and did a painting, *Walpole, 1972,* about the Massachusetts state prison where he was locked up. He showed convicts at Walpole moving around freely within their cellblock.

Keigney's painting called *Haircut, F-Ward* is a self-portrait of the artist getting a terrible haircut in Bridgewater, a Massachusetts correctional institution. "They sat me on a box," said Keigney, "and while playing cards, ran the clippers over my head, leaving little patches of hair, here and there, and they took me to the ward. I had a visit from my girlfriend later. She walked right past me, sitting there wearing the wrinkled, ill-fitting gray uniform, scuffed-up shoes about four sizes too big and curling up at the toes, gray socks that hung down over the shoe tops because the elastic was out. When I called to her and she saw me, she burst into tears."

A woman prisoner, Elaine Butler, did a picture of inmates at her facility lying outdoors on towels. She sarcastically called it *Mabel's Beach*. But the beach in her painting is actually a sunbathing area behind a high wire fence at the Mabel Bassett Correctional Center in Oklahoma. "No matter how high we rolled our shorts up or closed our eyes," said Butler, "we were still in prison."

Prisoners who draw directly from observation can get reported for misconduct. Tom Crochetiere, for example, carefully worked on an ink line drawing, *Behind the Wall,* of the view from his cell window. When he proudly showed it to a guard he knew, the guard said, "Very nice, but I will have to confiscate it." The guard thought that Crochetiere was planning an escape and took the drawing away. Crochetiere said, "I like to draw buildings and houses. I was disappointed I wouldn't be able to finish it. What stressed me the most was not having the freedom to draw what I wanted." However, Crochetiere was eventually given special permission to complete the drawing, and it was held for him until his release.

Crystal Stimpson, **Kidnapped.** *In the middle of the night women prisoners are marched into a van to be transferred to a different penitentiary.*

Some prisoners make artwork for other inmates, such as drawings, picture frames, painted handkerchiefs, and greeting cards—not as gifts, but as objects for sale. The payment comes this way: the convicts ordering the art use their vouchers at the canteen to get something the artists want—cigarettes, candy, or perhaps more art supplies.

Prisoners often carve sculptures out of soap. For tools they use Popsicle sticks, plastic forks, pencils, or even paper clips. Dominic Vincenzo-Thomas, doing twenty years to life for murder, makes delicate sculptures out of toilet paper. He began this craft when he was put into isolation and worked as a janitor. One time an inmate threw wet toilet paper at somebody else and it stuck to the wall. Vincenzo-

Arthur Keigney, **Haircut, F-Ward.** *The guard giving Keigney a haircut is so busy playing cards that he doesn't see that he has shaved off half of Keigney's hair. Keigney died in the prison infirmary while serving life without parole for a prison murder. After his death the case was thrown out and his codefendants were released.*

Thomas scraped it off and found that it was hard and kept its shape. So he began using toilet paper as a medium for sculpting. His most popular subjects, in demand by other convicts, were clowns, scarecrows, and hoboes. But sometimes he sculpted figures that had personal meanings. *Released by Death* is a portrait of an old convict who has intentionally overdosed on drugs and lies dying on his bed while listening to a Walkman.

Many jails allow art teachers to come in and offer programs. Phyllis Kornfeld, an art facilitator, wrote about her experiences in a book, *Cellblock Visions,* illustrated with works created by prisoners. Kornfeld wrote that she did not really teach art. She only supplied materials and encouragement. "If any of the prison artists here had had the opportunities and support that I enjoyed from an early age," she said, "I am certain that the great majority would not be locked up, meeting art for the first time behind bars, and when it may be too late."

BEHIND BARBED WIRE:
MINÉ OKUBO

Unlike outsider artists, Miné (pronounced mee-neh) Okubo

studied art. She was a young Japanese American woman born in Riverside, California. After receiving her master's degree from the University of California at Berkeley, Okubo went to Europe on a fellowship for more training. But when World War II broke out in 1939, she came home and went to work on a mosaic project in Oakland sponsored by the government. She also had a job as a docent in a museum. While Mexican artist Diego Rivera painted a mural,

she explained his art to visitors.

Miné and her brother Toku, a college student, shared a little house in Berkeley. On Sunday morning, December 7, 1941, they were listening to the radio when an announcer reported the news: the Japanese had bombed Pearl Harbor. "We were shocked," wrote Okubo. "We wondered what this would mean to us and the other people of Japanese descent in the United States." On December 8, the United States declared war on Japan, and three

days later it declared war on Germany and Italy. President Franklin D. Roosevelt issued Executive Order 9066, which gave government officials the authority to remove people of Japanese parentage from their homes and businesses and send them to "relocation centers."

Miné and Toku were ordered to leave for Tanforan Assembly Center, a former racetrack, in San Bruno, near San Francisco. "We had three days and three nights to pack and get ready," she wrote. From then on they were called by a number, 13660, rather than by their family name.

At Tanforan, along with thousands of other Japanese Americans, they went through a medical examination and were then led to their new home: a horse stable. They occupied Stall 50.

"Cameras and photographs were not permitted in the camps," wrote Okubo, "so I recorded everything in sketches, drawings, and paintings." She had brought along art supplies and began a series of pen-and-ink drawings intended for her friends, "to tell the story of camp

"Many of the women could not get used to the community toilets," wrote Miné Okubo as a caption for this drawing.

Okubo tries to keep order in the classroom, but some of her students fight and paint each other's faces.

life." She called her collection of drawings by her new name, *Citizen 13660.* Each page offers an episode of her experience illustrated in bold line drawings similar to Japanese woodblock prints. Shading and pattern are created by dots, dashes, and cross-hatching. Okubo appears somewhere in each scene, either in the foreground, off to the side sketching, or as part of the crowd.

The opening pages show Okubo and her brother arriving at Stall 50, setting up their cots, and sweeping away the dust and cobwebs with a whisk broom as they hold their noses and wipe away tears. Outside, they join the endless line for food. Okubo hugs herself against the cold, her wispy black hair blowing in the wind.

More drawings show the two of them filling their mattresses

Okubo pulls a blanket up to her chin as protection from "wild creatures."

with straw, lugging them back to their stall, and trying to get some sleep. Further on, a humorous drawing portrays Okubo in bed, confronting two mice perched on the frame of her cot. "We had to make friends with the wild creatures in the camp," she wrote, "especially the spiders, mice, and rats, because we were outnumbered." Another drawing illustrates the embarrassing lack of privacy in community bathrooms. Okubo also showed older women trying to take a bath. "It was a common sight to see them

bathing in pails, dishpans, or in tubs made from barrels," she wrote. Okubo documented every aspect of camp life: lineups at the post office; the mess hall, where "table manners were forgotten"; and a classroom in which she struggles to teach art to misbehaving children.

By September 1942, Miné and Toku were "relocated" to Topaz, a "permanent center" in Utah. The camp was in the middle of the desert. Okubo continued her pictorial saga and drew pictures of the bleak, dusty land-

scape, rows of barracks covered in tar paper, the small room she and her brother shared with a third person, a bleak Christmas, and a battle with mosquitoes in the summer. But she also illustrated enjoyable moments such as an exciting snowfall in October and visiting an art exhibit of crafts made by residents from odds and ends found in the camp.

A year later, in the fall of 1943, Okubo and others at Topaz had the opportunity to leave and return to their normal life. After answering questions concerning her allegiance to the United States and undergoing repeated loyalty checks, Okubo was free to go. Her last two drawings show her tearfully saying goodbye to her friends inside the gate, then getting into a car outside the barbed wire and leaving Topaz behind her. "My thoughts shifted from the past to the future," she wrote in her closing line.

Okubo moved to New York City, where she worked as an illustrator for *Fortune* magazine. And she took up painting again and exhibited her work. During her internment, she had created

Helga Weissová, **On the Toilet.** *This drawing illustrates the lack of hygiene facilities at Terezin. The prisoner wears a yellow star on her blouse.*

two thousand drawings about life in the camps. She published 206 of them in her book *Citizen 13660,* the first personal account of the internment camps.

BEHIND BARBED WIRE: HELGA WEISSOVÁ

In December 1941, when Helga Weissová had just turned twelve, she and her parents were forced to leave their home in Prague, Czechoslovakia. The Nazis had invaded Czechoslovakia and had come to power. They deported Weissová's family to the Terezin (Theresienstadt) concentration camp along with thousands of other Jews. Each person was only allowed to bring about a hundred pounds of belongings. Weissová had always loved to draw, so she packed art supplies: "a pad, a box of watercolours, crayons and pencils."

At Terezin, a former army fortress, Weissová and her mother stayed in a women's barracks, while her father was sent to a building for men. Weissová missed her father terribly and made her first drawing for him in bright colors. It was a pleasant winter scene of a boy and girl building a snowman. "I secretly smuggled this drawing to my father in the barracks," she recalled. "He wrote back: 'Draw what you see!'"

Weissová immediately changed her focus and muted her colors. "I felt called from now on to capture in my drawings the everyday life of the Ghetto," she wrote.

Helga Weissová, **Children Have Lessons.** Weissová drew a watercolor picture of children walking into one of the buildings at Terezin to study secretly.

Her next picture, *Arrival in Theresienstadt,* illustrated the two-mile walk from the train station to the camp. Prisoners wearing numbered tags and pale yellow Stars of David march under armed guard. Mothers hold babies, men lug briefcases and backpacks, and older people lean on canes.

Weissová moved into a "girls' home," L410, and painted a picture of the dormitory. She lived in Room 24 with about thirty-five girls her age. They slept on three-tiered bunks. Weissová's bunk was in the middle, near a window with a view of the street. "With my pad resting on my knees," she

*Helga Weissová, **Birthday Wish I.** This drawing illustrates Helga's dream of receiving a huge cake. "Where did it come from?" she wrote. "From Prague, of course." She included a picture of the Prague castle, the Hradschin.*

recalled, "I drew on this bunk everything I saw and experienced. I only did a few drawings outside, pictures in pencil on the spot of some of the streets and barracks courtyards." Grim street scenes show a woman scavenging in garbage to find something to eat and a man literally scraping the bottom of a barrel for food.

Just like Miné Okubo, Weissová kept a visual record of her life. She drew everything: people lining up for food, women trying to wash themselves with cold water, children attending makeshift classes.

However, at Terezin, school was forbidden. "Only lessons in drawing and crafts were permit-

ted," wrote Weissová. One of her watercolors shows children working, carrying benches into a building under the watchful eye of a "Ghetto cop" (page 19). But once inside, the children secretly "gathered together somewhere in a corner to learn."

A drawing dated December 1942 portrays children delivering

bread on a hearse, a wagon normally used for carrying coffins. "Everything was transported in old hearses," wrote Weissová. It was the only means of transportation allowed the prisoners, another way for the Nazis to dehumanize them.

On the Toilet (page 18) humorously depicts the plight of a young woman taking her turn in the bathroom. "The doors could not be locked," wrote Weissová, "and outside there were always people trying to force themselves in."

Lack of good hygiene facilities posed a constant danger. Diseases such as scarlet fever and typhoid swept through Terezin. On April 4, 1943, Weissová did a crayon drawing of a nurse carrying a bedpan past a door marked "Typhus!!" The same day Weissová repeated the drawing with greater definition in watercolor and pen-and-ink. *Hospital* shows the nurse in a section of the dormitory reserved for the seriously ill. Weissová painted it in drab shades of gray and green.

But when she drew pictures of her dreams and fantasies, she used bold, vivid colors. *Birthday Wish I* features well-dressed children bringing an enormous cake on a hearse from Prague to Terezin. "The most precious gift was food," wrote Weissová. In *Birthday Wish II,* she did a portrait of herself wearing a jaunty hiking outfit as she walks past a signpost, away from Terezin. The picture expressed her deepest desire: "going home to Prague."

When Weissová ran out of paper, her father managed to get her more from the studio where adult artist prisoners made graphs, charts, and posters. "She used to sit on her bed and draw and paint constantly," recalled Charlotte, the girl who slept on the bottom bunk.

Weissová became best friends with Franzi, the girl in the top bunk. They discovered that they had both been born in November 1929 in the same "maternity home" in Prague. As a gift for Franzi's fourteenth birthday, Weissová composed a picture in three parts, entwined by a painted ribbon. The section labeled "1929" commemorates their birth, "1943" illustrates the present, as represented by their bunk, and "1957" portrays them in the future wheeling baby carriages side by side. "Together we planned our future life after the War," wrote Weissová about this painting. "We imagined what it would be like in another fourteen years. We both will be mothers by then and will go for walks in Prague."

Franzi was deported to Auschwitz and died before her fifteenth birthday.

At Terezin everyone's worst fear was "transport to the east" and the Nazi death camps. "The summons to join the transport was distributed mostly at night," wrote Weissová. In a pencil drawing she captured the terror of a shadowy, silhouetted figure shining a flashlight on someone summoned in a top bunk.

Weissová and her mother were ordered to leave for the Auschwitz concentration camp in 1944, three days after her father was deported. Weissová left her collection of a hundred drawings with her uncle, who hid them. Any pictures of life at Terezin were forbidden.

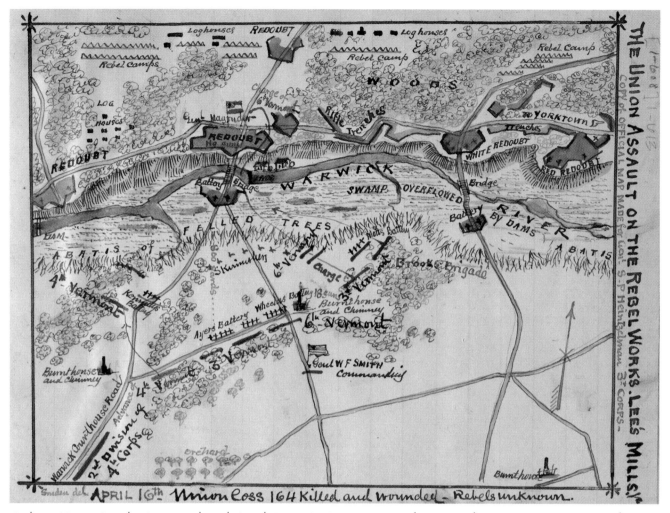

Within the map (as labeled): THE UNION ASSAULT ON THE REBEL WORKS. LEE'S MILLS. / Copy of official map made for Lieut. S. P. Heintzelman 3d CORPS.

Loghouses · REDOUBT · Loghouses · Rebel Camp · Rebel Camps · WOODS · Rebel Camp · LOG HOUSES · Charge of 6th Vermont · Genl. Maumdm · Rifle Trenches · TO YORKTOWN · Trenches · REDOUBT · WHITE REDOUBT · RED REDOUBT · Battery · Bridge · WARWICK · SWAMP OVERFLOWED · Bridge · Battery · RIVER · BY DAMS · ABATIS · DAM · FELLED TREES · ABATIS of · 4th Vermont · Skirmishers · 6th Vermont · Hex Nods Battery · Brooks Brigade · Charge of 3d Vermont · Ayers Battery · Wheelers Battery 18 guns · Burnt house and Chimney · 6th Vermont · Mott's Battery · Kennys Battery · Burnt house and chimney · 3d Vermont · Genl W F SMITH Commanding · 4th Vermont · Advance of 2d Division of 4th Corps · Warwick Courthouse Road · orchard · Burnt house · Sneden del · APRIL 16th Union Loss 164 killed and wounded — Rebels unknown.

Robert Knox Sneden's map dated April 16, 1862. His notes diagram the Union Army's attack. "They were received by the enemy with a crashing fire," he wrote, "which drove them back."

"If drawings were discovered," wrote Weissová, "the artists together with their families were sent to the Small Fortress. There they were murdered or hauled off to other concentration camps."

Weissová and her mother went from Auschwitz to Freiberg and Mauthausen, where they were liberated in May 1945 by American troops. When Weissová saw her uncle again, he returned the pictures to her, and she brought them back to Prague. Her father had died, but she and her mother moved into their old apartment. Weissová studied at the Academy of Fine Arts and became a professional artist. Later, she married a musician and they had three children, then grandchildren.

But to this day, Helga Weissová sleeps with the one hundred drawings of Terezin tucked under her bed.

BEHIND BATTLE LINES:
PRIVATE ROBERT KNOX SNEDEN

When the Civil War broke out in 1861, Robert Knox Sneden was working in New York City either as an engineering surveyor or as an apprentice architect. A bachelor, he lived with his parents and siblings and enjoyed painting watercolor sketches of sailboats on the Hudson River in his spare time. So when Sneden joined the 40th New York Volunteers of the Union Army in 1861, he continued sketching whenever he could. He had the same impulse that Miné Okubo and Helga Weissová had eighty years later: to document his wartime experiences through art.

Private Sneden sketched pictures of the various places where his regiment was stationed from New York to Virginia. He probably did all his drawings in pencil and pen-and-ink, then added color later. His commanding officer noticed his drawing skill and assigned him as a mapmaker for General Samuel P. Heintzelman in January 1862.

In March, Sneden, armed with his sketchbook, trudged through muddy roads with the general and drew battle plans as well as diagrams of battles that had just taken place. For example, a map dated April 16 illustrates the Union Army's attack on Rebel forces along the Warwick River near Lee's Mill, Virginia. On the bottom of the map Sneden wrote in script, "Union loss 164 killed and wounded—Rebels unknown."

As the Union Army marched south toward Richmond, Sneden made detailed "word pictures," sketches with captions or illustrations from his journal entries, of battlefields, towns, and houses occupied by the Union soldiers for military purposes. In July 1863, he learned about the Battle of Gettysburg in Pennsylvania. He pictured it in somber tones based on descriptions he heard and possibly on photographs he saw.

In October, Sneden went back into battle himself. He was assigned to make maps for

View of Sneden's shanty at Andersonville prison, Georgia, July 1864.

23

General William H. French of the Potomac Army. On November 26, 1863, Sneden moved to the general's headquarters in a house near Brandy Station, Virginia. The next day, just before dawn, when the general had already left with most of his men, Sneden was captured by Confederate soldiers. They forced him and a few other Union prisoners to ride bareback on mules to the train depot. Then the prisoners were shipped by train to Richmond, Virginia, where they were held briefly in a warehouse on Belle Island.

But Sneden kept sketching. "From the front windows I got a fine view of the Libby Prison," he wrote, and he drew a picture of it, including the gallows. "Scores of spies and deserters from the Rebel army recaptured were here hung in February," he noted.

Sneden left Richmond by prison train and rode in a cattle car. "The guards were on the roof," he wrote, "and on the ground twenty feet or so from the cars, with their muskets at a 'ready' to shoot any one of us who would try to escape. . . ."

On the night of February 28, they arrived at their final destination: the Andersonville, Georgia, prison camp.

It was an outdoor prison completely exposed to sun, rain, wind, and cold. Sneden's sketches, painted in muddy browns, show views from the outside and from

Sneden's portrait of Captain Henry Wirz, Confederate States of America jailor. All the prisoners at Andersonville hated Captain Wirz.

the inside. Prisoners had to build their own tents or shanties out of anything they could find: pine branches, sticks, mud from the swamp. Sneden illustrated the variety of tents, some covered

with "old tattered overcoats and ragged dirty blankets," others filled in with pine branches. "The whole camp looked like a collection of pig pens," he wrote. In a rough sketch Sneden portrayed his own shanty alongside other tents and burrows (holes dug in the ground and covered with branches), with prisoners "playing cards, cooking, dying alone."

Another scene, painted in washes of bluish gray and brown, shows a guard shooting a prisoner who has dared to take a piece of "the dead line" for firewood. The dead line, a low wooden fence encircling the entire camp, stood twenty feet inside the stockade walls. The jailor in charge, Captain Henry Wirz, had given orders that no prisoner could approach it nearer than ten or twelve feet or he would be shot. In a postwar drawing, Sneden portrayed Captain Wirz and labeled it "Demon of Andersonville."

Sneden's sketches offer other glimpses of Andersonville prison—ferocious dogs used to track down escaped prisoners, and "The Gallows," built to hang six prisoners dubbed "The Raiders," who were punished for robbing and killing "their weak and dying comrades." A vast panorama of the entire camp shows the "Hanging of the Raiders on July 11, 1864."

Sneden drew a map of Andersonville prison based on a pencil sketch. The plan includes specific details such as the outer walls of the stockade, the dead line inside, the swamp running through the camp, and the guards' camp and Captain Wirz's headquarters beyond.

On September 17, 1864, after spending seven months at Andersonville and surviving sickness and starvation, Sneden was moved to a new prison in Savannah, Georgia. From there he was sent to Camp Lawton. When Sneden promised not to try to escape, he was allowed to work as a clerk for a Confederate surgeon. But in his spare time he kept secretly sketching the places he observed.

In December 1864, Sneden was one of a large group of Union prisoners who were exchanged for Confederate prisoners. The mass exchange took place in Charleston Harbor. Sneden boarded a ship and headed for home. He arrived in New York City the day after Christmas, to the astonishment of his family, who thought he had died.

After a few months of rest, Sneden went to work for an architectural firm in New York, but he remained obsessed with the Civil War. He devoted the rest of his life to organizing and finishing his hundreds of watercolors, sketches, and maps. All together it made a vivid eyewitness account. In Sneden's own words, he left as a legacy "a good WAR RECORD."

From century to century, going back in time, prisoners who never knew each other had a universal experience. They felt driven to produce art despite the slim chances of their work surviving and ever being seen. Through their art they rose above hardships and left enduring accounts of their confinements.

chapter 3

Pattern for Freedom: Women's Quilts as Art

SLAVE QUILTS

Over the years, women have made quilts not only to produce something useful, but as a form of self-expression. They have needed beauty despite the ugliness of their surroundings. Women who could not even read or write have passed on their emotions, histories, and religious beliefs through quilting. Sometimes women have even fought back and resisted oppression with quilts. Many of their creations are so brilliantly original and beautiful that they are considered art.

Before the Civil War, African American slave women on plantations made quilts in their "spare time." That is, after the day's work was done or on Saturday afternoons and Sunday evenings. Children helped, too. "When I was a child at home," recalled one slave, "we never had no time to play. When we came in from the cotton fields, we'd have to start quiltin'." The slaves often stayed up all night finishing quilts for "the white folks." Another slave remembered getting burned. "Why, dey is a scar on my arm yet where my brother let de pine drip on me," he remembered. "Rich pine war all de light we ebber had. My brother was a holdin' de pine so's I can help mammy tack de quilt and he go to sleep and let it drop."

Sometimes the slaves worked with the mistress of the plantation, who taught them how to stitch and quilt. The quilts were used as blankets, coverlets, and crib quilts in the big house or as blankets for the slaves. Sometimes slaves used quilts as beds—they slept on the floor on a stack of quilts and covered themselves with more quilts. They had to make their own bed coverings by piecing together leftover scraps of cloth and padding the inner layer with cotton and cotton seeds.

The slaves made two kinds of quilts: some based on European American designs and others with their own patterns. Africans who had been captured and enslaved came from many countries and spoke different languages. They handed on their traditions by telling stories and making quilts. According to scholars, some African quilts communicate information in a secret code. A cross shaped like an X, for example, signifies a crossroads. Conveying messages this way was commonplace in African culture. Tribes that had no written language taught ancestral customs, events, and legends through textiles. The snake motif represented the West African god of fertility, and flower patterns symbolized the Haitian goddess of love. Slaves taught each other designs such as "Cotton Leaf," "Tulip," "Tree of Paradise," "Log Cabin in the Lane," and "Whirligig."

Many black quilt makers thought it boring to repeat the same design over and over, so they invented original patterns. The Crazy Quilt was started by a slave named Hannah in North Carolina. When Hannah was twelve years old, her master, John Logan, gave her to his daughter as a wedding gift. Logan also gave his new son-in-law a twelve-year-old slave boy named Pharoh. Hannah became a house servant and Pharoh became a blacksmith on the plantation. Later they married and had a daughter, Emma. Hannah made many quilts. One of her last was the Crazy Quilt. She died before it was done, and Emma completed it in 1895, stitching the words, "Finished by M."

A slave woman in Mississippi created patterns inspired by nature. Years later her daughter showed one particular quilt to a museum curator and told how it was made.

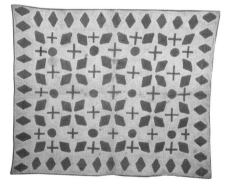

Crib quilt made between 1840 and 1860. The crosses and suns are symbols derived from the Bakongo tribe of central Africa.

A sixteen-year-old slave boy made this pieced quilt, embroidered with designs inspired by plants that grew where he lived.

This appliqué quilt with the embroidered date "March 19, 1852" was made by a slave called Yellow Bill, who sewed every stitch himself.

"My mother wove that white cloth an' the thread it's quilted with," she said. "The red an' green an' blue pieces was bought from the store, but she got the pattern by goin' out into the woods an' gettin' a leaf to cut it by. The two parts of the pattern is cut from the bull-tongue leaf and the gopher grass. The quilt is about ninety years old, an' it was made when people was smart, an' went into the woods to get their patterns."

Most slaves could not read or write. It was against the law to teach them. But they left a record of their lives in the quilts they designed. Their choices of bold color, odds and ends of fabric, and wild patterns expressed their feelings. Red, a favorite color, symbolized a woman's birth process and a man's role as hunter and warrior. Blue represented protection for the maker of the quilt. But superstitions went along with quilting. "Don't start to sew a piece of goods on Friday unless you are sure you can get it done before night, for that is bad luck," said one slave. And the color black often meant someone might die.

However, black later came to have a different meaning on the Underground Railroad. When runaway slaves trying to escape to the North saw a quilt with black fabric hanging on a clothesline or airing in a window, they knew they could safely stop at that house. If the popular "Log Cabin"

The "Drunkard's Path" pattern instructed runaway slaves to follow a crooked route.

design had a black square in the center instead of the usual red (representing a fireplace), it signaled a safe house. Other patterns, such as "Jacob's Ladder," sent the same signal. Quilts conveyed secret messages in the Underground Railroad Quilt Code.

One scholar learned about the code from an African American craftswoman, Mrs. Ozella McDaniel Williams, to whom the story had been passed down. Williams explained that different shapes gave traveling instructions. Quilts with zigzag patterns such as "Drunkard's Path" told escapees to take an indirect route and double back in order to escape slave catchers. "Drunkards weave back and forth, never moving in a straight line," Williams said. A star meant to follow the North Star. The "Flying Geese" pattern instructed the fleeing slaves to head north in the springtime, just like geese. Although the pattern has triangles pointing north, east, south, and west, the quilter made one set a different color, thus showing which way to go. Even the stitches told what paths to take. "The length of the stitches and the position of the stitches formed a language that only the slave would know," said Williams. The quilts became maps and helped many slaves escape to freedom.

NARRATIVE QUILTS: HARRIET POWERS

Harriet Powers, born a slave in 1837 in Athens, Georgia, made

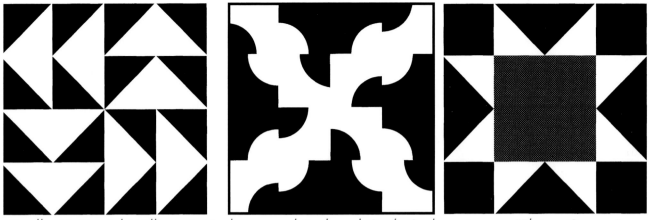

Ozella McDaniel Williams's Underground Railroad Quilt Code patterns: "Flying Geese," "Drunkard's Path," "Star/Evening Star/North Star."

narrative quilts, which told stories. She had learned how to sew from her mother. Powers married and at first made quilts just to keep her family warm. When slaves were freed officially by proclamation in 1863 and the Civil War ended in 1865, Harriet and her husband stayed near Athens. They farmed a few acres of their own land in Sandy Creek. After Powers had raised her children, she began making her first story quilt.

A deeply religious woman, she was inspired to sew panels depicting versions of stories from the Old Testament and the New Testament that she had heard and memorized through the years. One section shows Adam and Eve naming the animals in the Garden of Eden. Another represents an angel climbing a ladder to heaven in Jacob's dream. Other pictures illustrate the baptism of Christ, the Last Supper, and the Crucifixion. "We can't go back no further than the Bible," said Powers.

She chose a method called appliqué. Although many cultures have used this technique in needlework, her designs showed a West African influence. Powers cut out cloth figures such as people, animals, birds, and stars, then stitched them onto the background fabric. She separated the panels with broken vertical strips, a motif reflecting a West African belief that "evil travels in straight lines." Crooked lines would scare away evil spirits.

When Powers finished her first quilt, she exhibited it at the Cotton Fair in Athens. Jennie Smith, a local painter and art teacher, spotted the quilt and immediately recognized its originality and beauty. "It is impossible to describe the gorgeous coloring of the work," Smith wrote later. She offered to buy the quilt but Powers refused to sell. However, a few years later, Powers and her husband needed money and she sold the quilt to Smith for five dollars. Smith promised to let Powers come back and visit the "darling offspring of my brain." Powers couldn't read or write, but she explained the stories she had

Harriet Powers's first story quilt. The section in the top left corner shows Adam and Eve naming animals in the Garden of Eden.

stitched in each picture and Smith wrote down her exact words.

Smith exhibited the quilt in the Negro Building at the 1895 Cotton States Exposition in Atlanta. Faculty ladies from At-lanta University saw and admired it, and they commissioned Powers to make a second quilt as a gift for Reverend Charles Cuthbert Hall, chairman of the board of trustees.

Powers's second quilt told sto-ries about heroes from the Bible—Noah, Jonah, and Job—who had successfully struggled against great odds. She also in-terpreted extraordinary cosmic events. One square depicts "the

Harriet Powers's second story quilt. The section about a runaway hog named Betts is in the middle of the bottom row. "The dark day of May 19, 1780" is the second square in the top row.

dark day of May 19, 1780," she said. "The seven stars were seen at 12 N. [noon] in the day." People thought the world was coming to an end and didn't realize until later that the eerie darkness was due to pollution from forest fires in New England.

Another section shows "The red light night of 1846. A man tolling the bell to notify the peo-ple of the wonder." The red lights were actually showers of shooting stars that Powers herself may have seen when she was eight years old. And another panel illustrates a tall tale about a hog named Betts who supposedly ran five hundred miles from Georgia to Virginia. Betts—an "independent hog," according to Powers—ran away to punish her rich owners, but may have also symbolized a slave's escape through the Under-ground Railroad.

It took Powers three years to make the quilt. During this time her husband left her and moved to another farm, but Powers sup-ported herself, earning a little extra money from sewing. In 1911, she died, almost penniless. Reverend Hall bequeathed Powers's quilt to

Essie Bendolph Pettway's "Pinwheel" variation. Several pieces in the quilt are scraps from dresses Essie made for herself and her mother.

his son, who later sold it to a folk-art collector. Today the quilt belongs to the Museum of Fine Arts in Boston. And Powers's first story quilt, which she called "A Sermon in Patchwork," is in the Smithsonian Institution's National Museum of American History in Washington, D.C. Powers's two Bible quilts live on as treasured works of art.

THE QUILTS OF GEE'S BEND

Women descended from slaves on the Pettway plantation in Gee's Bend, Alabama, have been making quilts "the old way" since the 1920s. Their designs feature abstract stripes, blocks, and geometric patterns such as "Log Cabin" in unusual combinations of bold colors. The women simply use scraps of leftover material.

Loretta Pettway, creator of a quilt in 1963 called "Housetop," in shades of taupe, gold, and turquoise, said, "I made all my quilts out of old shirts and dress tails and britches legs. I couldn't never get no good fabric to make quilts, so I had to get the best of the old clothes my peoples wore or old clothes I got from other peoples. . . . I ain't never made a real pattern. I just made what my grandmama had made back in those days— 'Bricklayer,' 'Housetop,' and stuff."

In the 1950s, Amelia Bennett made a quilt of asymmetrical blocks and strips of cloth in purple and bright red, with a flower pattern of red, blue, and turquoise. Some of the pieces are thin cotton, others are corduroy. "I was eleven years old and I used to watch my mother when she pieced quilts," Bennett recalled, "and I would pick up all the little pieces and watch her sew them together. And I kept doing that until I got a big part. And she say, 'Honey, you doing good.' So then she give me some pieces. She say, 'You understand how to cut them?'

"I say, 'I'm going to try.'

"She say, 'Well, if you try you can make it.'

"I kept a-doing that till I pieced up the whole top. . . . What I first did, I showed it to my daddy, and he was amazed over me making it. From then on all the strips my mother give them to me, and I kept mending them together till I got a quilt top. . . . And on and on and on,

Loretta Pettway's "Housetop" (top) is made of "the best of the old clothes my peoples wore . . . like the back of the pants legs, 'cause the knees mostly be wore out. We pick the cotton on our knees."

Mary L. Bennett's "Housetop" quilt (bottom) repeats variations of the pattern in different colors. "Didn't nobody teach me to make quilts," she said. "I just learned it by myself, about twelve or thirteen."

I just kept piecing up and kept quilting."

Sometimes the women work together in a quilting bee and sing spirituals and church hymns as they stitch. They love music, and they also enjoy keeping each other company. But Nettie Young said, "In the quilting bee time, I started using patterns, but I shouldn't have did it. It broke the ideas I had in my head. I should have stayed with my own ideas."

On her own Young created a "Milky Way" quilt in 1971 that features powerful black and white circles and squares within frames of red and gray.

Essie Bendolph Pettway's "Pinwheel" quilt, sewn in 2000, explodes with color. Rectangles and triangles range from solid dark green to a bright green leaf pattern and contrasting shades of blue and turquoise. Bendolph Pettway said, "Maybe I was twelve or thirteen when I made my first quilt. I have a family with a lot of peoples quilting . . . and I picked up a lot from watching them and learning what they was doing. . . . I get pleasure from my quilts. I enjoy seeing other peoples enjoying my work."

The quilts of Gee's Bend were recently collected for an exhi-

bition put on jointly by the Museum of Fine Arts, Houston, and the Tinwood Alliance. The exhibit then traveled to the Whitney Museum of American Art in New York City and opened to rave reviews. "Eye-poppingly gorgeous," wrote a critic for the *New York Times*. "Some of the most miraculous works of modern art America has produced."

Against all odds, African American women quilters descended from slaves have preserved and continued a rich heritage.

chapter 4
Kids Create Art Against the Odds...

TIM ROLLINS AND K.O.S.

In 1981, artist Tim Rollins took a job teaching in the special-education department of a junior high school in the South Bronx, New York City. The area, once a middle-class neighborhood full of traditional families, had become a ghetto. It resembled a war zone. Apartment buildings had been burned to ruins. Drug addicts camped out in the empty shells of the buildings. Graffiti covered the walls.

Rollins's students, ages eleven to fifteen, lived in this run-down environment, where violence was an everyday occurrence. They all were handicapped in some way: some had emotional problems, others were learning-disabled. The school had hired two other teachers in the past two years, and Rollins was their last hope. "The South Bronx is considered incapable of creating beauty," said Rollins. "I was immediately struck by how many of my 'problem' students possessed genuine talent, interest, and volition when they were involved in art. It was also obvious that forcing the students to conform to a traditional art-class schedule and curriculum would not work."

Rollins wanted to introduce the kids to classic literature, a seemingly impossible task. "For kids, books were the enemy," he said. When he handed out copies of George Orwell's *1984* and asked them to draw while he read aloud, they misunderstood and started drawing directly on the pages of their books. The kids got excited about what

Tim Rollins in his signature black hat with members of K.O.S.

they had done, and so did Rollins. Rather than scolding them for defacing books, he realized that they had hit on an innovative new art form. Together they applied the pages of the text to canvas and began working collectively on a large-scale composition. This process of creating images over text as a group became their way of making art.

"By 1982," said Rollins, "our classroom, Room 318, had been transformed into a working studio for young artists. . . . I made my art with the kids—during classes, during free periods, during lunch periods, in the short time after school allowed us before getting kicked out by the custodians." The core group of young people who worked with Rollins called themselves K.O.S. (Kids of Survival).

Soon Rollins needed a bigger space without restrictions. He found an abandoned gym in another Bronx school, got a grant from the National Endowment for the Arts, and formed a non-profit organization called The Art & Knowledge Workshop. By 1987, he gave up teaching in public school and devoted himself exclusively to creating art with kids from the ghetto.

Some didn't stick with him. They drifted away and turned to drugs or became teenage mothers and fathers. Rollins established his rules: the kids had to be enrolled in school and not be parents. "No dropouts. No babies," he said. But the kids who stayed produced powerful paintings inspired by texts such as Nathaniel Hawthorne's *The Scarlet Letter,* Stephen Crane's *The Red Badge of Courage,* George Orwell's *Animal Farm,* and Franz Kafka's *Amerika.* Rollins wanted the kids to grasp the books and respond emotionally. "Classic themes speak to them," he said, and stressed the importance of reading for an artist.

"We have a chance to make a statement," said George Graces, a member of K.O.S., "and for people our age, this is a big chance. We paint what is, but we also paint what should be."

Richie Cruz said, "I guess art is one of the only ways we can show

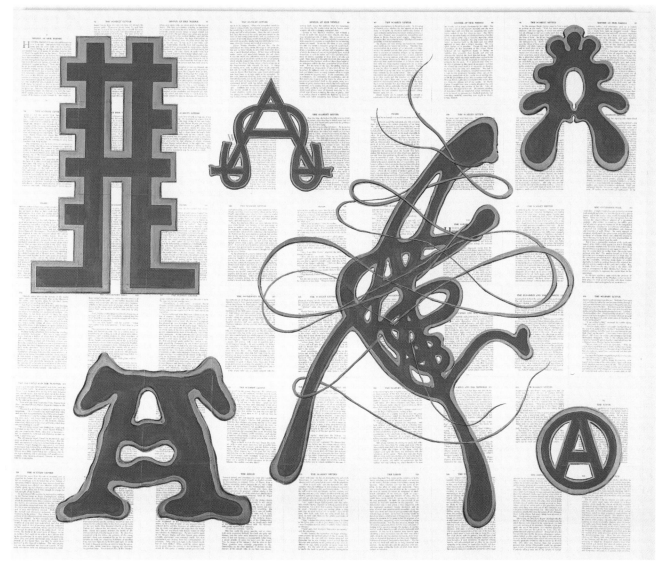

Tim Rollins and K.O.S., **Hester at Her Needle,** *inspired by* **The Scarlet Letter.**

our point of view, about how we see the world. We don't own a TV station, but we can get a painting together."

"The kids research the text," said Rollins, "and find the inspirational moment." For example,

in 1985 he read them the last chapter of Kafka's unfinished novel *Amerika,* about an imaginary version of America called Amerika. The main character, a sixteen-year-old immigrant named Karl, has come to the New World but

feels that he's a failure. Just as he's about to go home, he arrives at "The Nature Theatre of Oklahoma . . . where everyone can be an artist, everyone is welcome." Karl decides to join and that night goes to register at the racetrack.

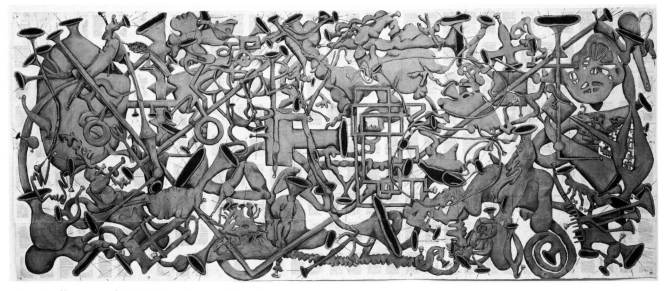

Tim Rollins and K.O.S., **Amerika I.**

"As he approaches," explained Rollins, "he hears this incredible sound of a traffic jam, and it's hundreds of horns, like a jazz orchestra or something. And . . . he sees hundreds of people standing on pedestals, dressed up like angels, blowing whatever they want to on these long golden horns. . . . Karl says, 'What is this?' and the guy says, 'This is Amerika, where everyone has a voice and everyone can say what they want.' "

Then Rollins said to *his* kids, "If you could be a golden instrument, if you could play a song of your freedom and dignity and your future and everything you feel about Amerika and this country,

what would your horn look like?"

The results, recalled Rollins, were "startling, explosive." Over a period of months, the kids designed all kinds of horns—curved, straight, fantastic. Then he selected a number of the horns, and together they transferred them to an enormous piece of heavy rag paper, six feet by fifteen feet, onto which Rollins had glued all the pages of Kafka's novel. The last step was painting the composition. The result was *Amerika I,* a signature piece for K.O.S. Since then new groups of kids have redone the same theme.

Rollins takes the kids to museums and exhibits to see works

by professional artists. So when K.O.S. worked on the text of *Alice's Adventures in Wonderland,* they were inspired by conceptual artist Ad Reinhardt, who paints an entire canvas in one color. Twelve-year-old Annette Rosado thought of Alice as a character who grows too big for her space. Rosado wanted to use red to express this feeling. "The Red Alice means both anger and blood to me," she said. "This is funny because red is also the color of love—like valentines. The Red Alice is a young girl who is so angry and in pain that she has had it and might jump out of the painting and fight back."

Nowadays Rollins no longer

allows girls in K.O.S. Too often they followed their boyfriends to the workshop and distracted them. "Times have changed," he explains. So he works with girls separately, as he did recently in Portland, Maine. Rollins conducts workshops with young people all over the world—Sweden, Israel, Australia, Ireland, England. When he led a group in Santa Monica, California, over a three-day period, they interpreted a scene from Shakespeare's *Midsummer Night's Dream,* as the girls in Maine had done. The girls had printed lithographs in shades of black with spray plastic glitter, but the kids in Santa Monica used color. At the end Rollins signed each painting alongside his students' signatures, and the works were displayed at the Santa Monica Museum of Art. Rollins told the kids to take care of their pictures and frame them. He had only one request: "Just don't sell them on eBay."

Works by Tim Rollins and K.O.S. belong to the collections of the Hirshhorn Museum in Washington, D.C., the Museum of Modern Art in New York, and the Tate Gallery in London, to name just a few. Their art travels throughout the world and is displayed in other museums and galleries. Many of the original members of K.O.S. have gone on to college and have become professional artists and teachers themselves.

Rollins's goal for the future? A new South Bronx Academy of Art. His credo is a quote from Dostoyevsky: "Only beauty can change things."

NOT SOLD IN STORES

In May 2000, Dr. John Schultz visited a fishing village at Lake Turkana, a saltwater lake in Kenya. Schultz, president of the Christian Children's Fund (CCF), was there to help villagers during a drought and famine. He had spent the last two days touring "scenes of devastation" in northwest Kenya. "I was expecting to see children and their families either begging or sitting idly by the side of the road waiting for their fate," he recalled. But when he came to the village at Lake Turkana, "it was quite a different atmosphere." As Schultz walked toward the lake, he heard the laughter of children and saw a group of young boys sailing toy boats. "I was struck by the fact that they were having a childhood, in spite of the famine and emergency at hand," he said.

"Having done a bit of sailing myself, I noticed that the boats were actually tacking and jibing, sailing from one child to another." Schultz made eye contact with one boy in particular, five-year-old Thomas Akimat Ekiru. Schultz stooped down and began to look carefully at the boy's boat. Thomas had made it from an old flip-flop sandal, two sticks, string

Thomas with his toy boat.

from a grain bag distributed by an aid organization, and a plastic bag. With gestures and sign language, Schultz admired the boat. "Then Thomas lifted up his boat and gave it to me," recalled Schultz. "I was very moved by this gesture." A worker accompanying Schultz who spoke Turkana asked the boy, "Are you giving this boat to this man?" And through the translator Thomas said to Schultz, "You can have it."

Schultz carried the boat home. "I now have it as a piece of art on my desk," he said. "Subsequently an idea dawned on me." Within

the next few months he ordered a motor-powered fiberglass boat to be delivered to Thomas's family. Schultz knew that they would use it with five or six other families because the villagers fished in groups. The fast new boat would enable them to bring a catch to shore quickly, where they could either eat it right away or cut it in strips and dry it, their only means of preservation.

But Thomas's gift gave Schultz another idea. He asked directors of CCF projects around the world to send him toys made by children. When CCF brought food and

medical aid to impoverished families suffering from disasters, things such as plastic bottles, bottle caps, and pesticide cans got thrown away, but children still found them usable. The result was an exhibit called "Not Sold in Stores: The Spirit of Childhood and the Power of Play." The exhibit included approximately 250 toys—balls, dolls, trucks—made from trash by children who needed to play despite living in appalling circumstances.

Some of the toys were crafted from local produce. For example, Teodoro, a ten-year-old in Honduras, made an *enchute,* a kind of "catch the ball on a stick" toy, from a fruit that grows on the jicara tree. When the fruit fell off the tree, he cleaned and scraped it, punched holes in it, and dried it in the sun. Then he hung his new hardened ball from a pointed stick with a string. He played with it by swinging the ball out as far as it would go and spearing it with the attached stick.

One of the toys chosen for the exhibit is a green cardboard man wearing a hat and holding the Sierra Leonean flag. It was made by a fourteen-year-old boy living

Snake toy made from bottle caps by Marta Alicia Gutierrez.

in a refugee camp. When the strings of the cardboard man are pulled, he shoots up his arms and kicks out his legs to dance. Jonah Davidson, director of the CCF in Sierra Leone, demonstrated how the toy worked as he sang, "Sally Wansai, Sally Wansai. Do you know Sally Wansai? Come and see Sally Wansai."

"*Wansai* means 'broken,'" explained Davidson. "Sally Wansai . . . is a common toy made by children in Sierra Leone. It's made from cardboard, wire, and some strings. You can shape it into a male or female. All parts of the body are connected by pieces of wire. When the kids play with it, they sing the song."

A popular toy from Africa and Latin America is a homemade soccer ball. David, a seven-year-old in Kenya, created one by wrapping layers of plastic bags and tying them with heavy string. Although the ball is smaller than a regulation model, David can kick it and use it in a game. Another boy in Guatemala did the exact same thing. His soccer ball was so well made that it lasted for a whole game. Schultz was there, and at the end of the game when he asked to

have the ball for the exhibit, he gave the boy a leather one in exchange.

In Zambia, a boy made a miniature bicycle out of wire left over from construction sites. He wrapped the wheels in cloth, and they really go around.

Basant, a nine-year-old in India, shaped an elephant from dried leaves, a coconut husk, and thread. In Honduras, Marta Alicia Gutierrez, age five, created a toy snake that wriggles across the floor when a string is pulled. She made the snake from more than a hundred metal bottle tops pierced with holes and threaded together. Teresa, a seventeen-year-old Angolan, created a spoon doll as a gift for her little sister. She dressed the cooking spoon with leftover fabric from the sleeve of a blouse.

Nalubuga, an eleven-year-old girl who lives in a mud hut in Kampala, Uganda, constructed a dollhouse from cardboard and banana-leaf fiber. The doors and windows of the yellow house open. Nalubuga put little figures inside but hardly any furniture. She wrote a note in the third person saying, "This is her dream house."

The exhibit opened at the

Simon Wiesenthal Center—Museum of Tolerance in Los Angeles in March 2001, then traveled to other venues, including the United Nations Visitors' Lobby in New York City. The display attracted so much interest while in the United States that it is still on tour. "The toys show the creativity of the children," said Robert L. Smythers of CCF. "Their minds are really, really working."

Newspapers published feature stories about the exhibit and printed pictures of some of the children, including Thomas and his boat. Schultz went back to Lake Turkana and showed Thomas his picture in the paper. Thomas was thrilled. "He showed it around to his friends." Today Schultz sponsors Thomas. They exchange letters every couple of months. "I write in English," said Schultz, "and a social worker translates and reads my letter to him." Thomas goes to school part-time and is learning to be a fisherman like his father. "The kids are still making flip-flop boats to learn the art of sailing," said Schultz. "Children are doing what children do in the most desperate circumstances in a creative way."

A portrait of Nene Humphrey, daughter-in-law of the artist George Andrews, known as "the Dot Man." With his typical swirl of dots and other marks, Andrews portrayed Nene reading.

Dr. John Schultz carried Thomas Akimat Ekiru's flip-flop sailboat home and said, "I now have it as a piece of art on my desk." Schultz regards a toy made from trash as a work of art. How do people know what is truly art? They can tell by their feelings. Viewers react to an object or painting with pleasure, sadness, anger, or even disgust. Art has the power to make people think and see the world in a new way. David Hockney, the renowned artist, once said, "Art is about sharing; you wouldn't be an artist unless you wanted to share an experience, a thought."

Art means surprises, originality, discoveries. A great number of works of art created against the odds were not discussed in this book, simply for lack of space. For instance, bullet casings painted with tiny flowers and miniature animals by Margit Winkler, a prisoner in Nazi concentration camps during World War II; the Watts Towers, constructed in Los Angeles by Simon Rodia; family portraits and bowls, trays, and porch furniture painted by farmer and outsider artist George Andrews, known as "the Dot Man"; and whirligigs created by Matteo Radoslovich in New Jersey, David Holzman in Tucson, and David Butler in New Orleans.

Older people often make art from their memories. Children create art as direct responses to their daily lives. Some professional artists and critics think of these kinds of art as the most pure because they are spontaneous and not influenced by training or knowledge of art history.

Painful experiences inspire the creation of art. Expressing pain in a drawing, painting, or collage helps the artist to heal. When terrorists attacked New York City in 2001, many children responded by making pictures to express their emotions, too horrified to put their feelings into words. Some of the art was gathered and exhibited at the Museum of the City of New York. Tim Rollins, teacher and leader of K.O.S. (Kids of Survival), said, "The works are living testimonies to the power of art to save histories, minds, and lives. Art, especially the art of children, is an act of hope."

A view of the Watts Towers, created by Simon Rodia.

Whirligig by David Butler called **Windmill with Rooster.** [Collection American Folk Art Museum, New York]

resources & references

SOME PLACES WHERE YOU CAN SEE ALL KINDS OF ART

Street fairs

County fairs

Local museums

Folk-art centers

Craft shows

History museums

University and library galleries

Auctions

Flea markets

Antiques and collectibles markets

Thrift stores

AND IF YOU'RE TRAVELING, YOU MAY BE ABLE TO VISIT THESE PLACES

American Folk Art Museum, New York, NY
(www.folkartmuseum.org)

American Visionary Art Museum, Baltimore, MD
(www.avam.org)

California African American Museum, Los Angeles, CA
(www.caam.ca.gov)

Cedarburg Cultural Center, Cedarburg, WI
(www.cedarburgculturalcenter.org)

Creative Growth Art Center, Oakland, CA
(www.creativegrowth.org)

Kentucky Art and Craft Foundation Gallery, Louisville, KY
(www.kentuckycrafts.org)

Kentucky Folk Art Center, Morehead, KY
(www.kyfolkart.org)

Morris Museum of Art, Augusta, GA
(www.themorris.org)

Museum of Fine Arts, Houston, TX
(www.mfah.org)

Shelburne Museum, Shelburne, VT
(www.shelburnemuseum.org)

Simon Wiesenthal Center—Museum of Tolerance, Los Angeles, CA
(www.museumoftolerance.com)

Smithsonian American Art Museum, Washington, DC
(www.nmaa.si.edu)

Smithsonian National Museum of American History, Washington, DC
(www.americanhistory.si.edu)

Vermont Quilt Festival, Northfield, VT
(www.vqf.org)

Watts Towers, Los Angeles, CA
(www.wattstowers.net)

BOOKS

(★)Denotes books suitable for younger readers.

Beardsley, John, ed. *The Quilts of Gee's Bend*. Atlanta: Tinwood Books, 2002.

★Bial, Raymond. *The Underground Railroad*. Boston: Houghton Mifflin, 1995.

Bobo, Jacqueline, ed. *Black Feminist Cultural Criticism*. Malden, MA: Blackwell Publishers, 2001.

★Bryan, Charles F. Jr., James C. Kelly, and Nelson D. Lankford, eds. *Images from the Storm: Private Robert Knox Sneden*. New York: The Free Press, 2001.

Eisen, George. *Children and Play in the Holocaust: Games Among the Shadows*. Amherst, MA: The University of Massachusetts Press, 1988.

*Fleischman, Paul. *Whirligig*. New York: Henry Holt and Company, 1998.

Frederickson, Kristen, and Sarah E. Webb, eds. *Singular Women: Writing the Artist*. Berkeley, CA: University of California Press, 2003.

*Fry, Gladys-Marie. *Stitched from the Soul: Slave Quilts from the Antebellum South*. 2nd ed. Chapel Hill, NC: The University of North Carolina Press, 2002.

*Goodman, Robin F., and Andrea Henderson Fahnestock. *The Day Our World Changed: Children's Art of 9/11*. New York: Harry N. Abrams, 2002.

Gruber, J. Richard. *The Dot Man: George Andrews of Madison, Georgia*. Augusta, GA: Morris Museum of Art, 1994.

Heinrich, Tanya, ed. *The Art of Adolf Wölfli: St. Adolf-Giant-Creation*. New York: American Folk Art Museum, 2003.

Hill, Kimi Kodani, ed. *Topaz Moon: Chiura Obata's Art of the Internment*. Berkeley, CA: Heyday Books, 2000.

*Kallen, Stuart A. *Life on the Underground Railroad*. San Diego: Lucent Books, 2000.

Kornfeld, Phyllis. *Cellblock Visions: Prison Art in America*. Princeton, NJ: Princeton University Press, 1997.

*Lyons, Mary E. *Stitching Stars: The Story Quilts of Harriet Powers*. New York: Charles Scribner's Sons, 1993.

MacGregor, John M. *Henry Darger: In the Realms of the Unreal*. New York: Delano Greenidge Editions, 2002.

★Okubo, Miné. *Citizen 13660.* Seattle and London: University of Washington Press, 1998. Originally published: New York, Columbia University Press, 1946.

Paley, Nicholas. *Finding Art's Place.* New York: Routledge, 1995.

Parkett Verlag. "Collaboration: Tim Rollins + K.O.S." *Parkett,* no. 21 (1989).

Rhodes, Colin. *Outsider Art: Spontaneous Alternatives.* London: Thames & Hudson, 2000.

★Roberts-Davis, Tanya. *We Need to Go to School: Voices of the Rugmark Children.* Toronto: Groundwood Books/Douglas & McIntyre, 2001.

★Sawyer, Kem Knapp. *The Underground Railroad in American History.* Springfield, NJ: Enslow Publishers, 1997.

Sellen, Betty-Carol, with Cynthia J. Johanson. *Self Taught, Outsider, and Folk Art: A Guide to American Artists, Locations and Resources.* Jefferson, NC: McFarland & Company, 1999.

Spoerri, Elka, ed. *Adolf Wölfli: Draftsman, Writer, Poet, Composer.* Ithaca, NY, and London: Cornell University Press, 1997.

★Tobin, Jacqueline L., and Raymond G. Dobard. *Hidden in Plain View: A Secret Story of Quilts and the Underground Railroad.* New York: Doubleday, 1999.

★Weissová, Helga. *Draw What You See: A Child's Drawings from Theresienstadt.* Göttingen, Germany: Wallstein Verlag, 1998.

WEB SITE

www.christianchildrensfund.org

VIDEOS

Against the Odds: The Artists of the Harlem Renaissance. Trenton, NJ: New Jersey Network, 1994.

Kids of Survival: The Art and Life of Tim Rollins & K.O.S. San Francisco: Geller/Goldfine Productions, 1998.

Terezin Diary. New York: First Run/Icarus Films, 1990.

Theresienstadt: Gateway to Auschwitz. Teaneck, NJ: Ergo Media, 1993.

Voices of the Children. New York: The Cinema Guild, 1996.

INTERVIEWS BY THE AUTHOR

1. Helga Weissová, in person at Moravian College in Bethlehem, PA, February 2000, and over the phone, May 2002 and May 2003.
2. Tim Rollins, in person in his Chelsea studio in New York City, February 2003.
3. Dr. John Schultz, over the phone, March 2003.

author bio

Susan Goldman Rubin is the author of many wonderful, award-winning books for children, including *Fireflies in the Dark: The Story of Friedl Dicker-Brandeis and the Children of Terezin; Margaret Bourke-White: Her Pictures Were Her Life; The Yellow House: Vincent van Gogh & Paul Gauguin Side by Side; Degas and the Dance: The Painter and the <u>Petits Rats</u>, Perfecting Their Art; Steven Spielberg: Crazy for Movies;* and *Searching for Anne Frank: Letters from Amsterdam to Iowa.* A graduate of Oberlin College, she lives in Malibu, California.